# Rea

## How to discover and appreciate its riches

by
Petroc Willey

*All booklets are published thanks to the
generous support of the members of the
Catholic Truth Society*

CATHOLIC TRUTH SOCIETY
PUBLISHERS TO THE HOLY SEE

# Contents

**Images:** Page 6: Icon of *Madonna and Child*, Basilica of the Annunciation © Zvonimir Atleticl / Shutterstock.com; page 16: Cathedral of Monreale, Sicily © Andreas Zerndl / Shutterstock.com; page 36: *The Trinity* (oil on panel), Baco, J. (1410-61) and Rexach, J. (1415-84) / Musee de Picardie, Amiens, France / Bridgeman Images; page 50: *Christ and the Apostles*, (I am the Life), Greek School, (17th century) / Byzantine Museum, Athens, Greece / De Agostini Picture Library / G. Dagli Orti / Bridgeman Images.

*ISBN 978 1 78469 102 8*

# INTRODUCTION

This booklet has been written to help you to appreciate and to enjoy with peaceful certainty the unchanging truths of the Catholic faith, presented to us for our time in the *Catechism of the Catholic Church*.

This *Catechism* was approved with the authority of all of the bishops of the world in union with Pope St John Paul II and under the direction of the future Pope Benedict XVI.[1] Not only does it represent the mind and heart of the Catholic Church at the start of the third millennium, it also provides us with the face of the Church throughout her Tradition, from the time of the apostles and their successors, with a text that draws from popes, saints, Church Councils and the liturgy.

The purpose of this work, then, is to facilitate the reading of the *Catechism* by drawing attention to its purpose and intended use, as well as its key features. You will find it most helpful if you have a copy of the *Catechism* with you when reading this short work. This will enable you to take your own journey of discovery through its pages.

You will notice that in this booklet each chapter is divided into sub-sections. These all seek to answer the overarching question, "What is the *Catechism* for?" The answers are given in these headings. It is written "to help us...", "to develop in us...", "to provide for us...", "to form us...", "to prepare us...", and so forth. These sub-headings also reveal what the *Catechism* will be doing for *you* when you read it, for it has been designed to help you in many formative ways through its presentation of the saving doctrines of the Church. "Doctrine" simply means "teaching". The Church teaches what she has received from Christ; she has received these doctrines to be passed on to you as lights along your path through life.

Doctrine is truth. It is not truth that can be separated from pastoral care, it is truth from the only one who can set us free; it is truth for freedom. This truth liberates and draws us into God's merciful love; it is truth for happiness. There is no real freedom or happiness without it. That is the importance of the *Catechism* for our lives. Read every paragraph of the *Catechism* slowly as truth to enlighten you, to free you, to strengthen you and to draw you into the wonder of God's love for you and for the whole world.

At the end of each chapter you will find an exercise that provides you with an opportunity to consolidate your understanding of the chapter. I would encourage you not to skip over these. They are valuable opportunities to enjoy your own reading of the text of the *Catechism*.

This booklet will help you, above all, to discover the centre of the *Catechism*'s presentation of the faith: the unceasing and saving love of the sacred heart of Jesus Christ. This is the reality to which the authors of the *Catechism* wish especially to draw our attention, for the love of Christ lies at the centre of the Church, of her teaching and her liturgy, her life and her prayer. The *Catechism* has been carefully and beautifully crafted in order to make this living centre luminous for us.[2] As we contemplate and learn more about the Person of Christ through our reading of the *Catechism* we will find that he leads us into a deep adoration of the Blessed Trinity, the source of all of the mysteries that make up God's plan of love for mankind and for the whole of creation.

# 1

# THE CHARACTER
# OF THE *CATECHISM*:
## an Annunciation

The *Catechism* is an annunciation for our times of the Good News of Jesus Christ. The annunciation of this Good News "of great joy"[3] with which we are most familiar was made, of course, by the archangel Gabriel to the Blessed Virgin Mary. It is the news that God himself would be born of her. She responded, "Be it done to me according to your word".[4] It is no coincidence that this response of Mary's, made at the dawn of our salvation, is one of the most cited scriptural references in the *Catechism*, for it beautifully sums up the response that the text of the *Catechism* seeks to elicit from each and every reader whenever the *Catechism* is opened and read.

## To help us respond to the gift of the Father

The heart of the Christian faith lies in this: that at the turning point of time and of history, a message of inexpressible hope was brought from God the Father by the angel Gabriel to the Blessed Virgin Mary, the one whom the *Catechism* describes as "the most humble of creatures".[5] The message announced the gift of God the Father's eternal Word who, at the lowest point of the ages, was to come from heaven to save us:

> For while gentle silence enveloped all things,
> and night in its swift course was now half gone,
> thy all-powerful word leaped from heaven,
>> from the royal throne,
> into the midst of the land that was doomed.[6]

It is this same message, of Christ and of the redemption he has won for us, that the *Catechism* brings to us today. And we are invited to respond with our own *fiat* to this Good News. In a way that is analogous to the annunciation by the angel to Mary, there is an overshadowing by the Holy Spirit that brings Christ to birth in us through our acts of faith today. For while the historic fact of the Incarnation - wherein the divine Son assumed human nature, taking flesh from Mary the Mother of God, in order to unite to himself all that in us is in need of healing and restoration - is unique,[7] never to be repeated, this unique event has also been seen by the Church in her holy Tradition as the paradigm for understanding *every reception* of the Word in our lives. Using this analogy of Christ's coming to birth in us, Pope St John Paul II spoke of the Church's work of catechesis as that of seeking to develop an "understanding of the mystery of Christ in the light of God's word, so that the whole of a person's humanity is impregnated by that word."[8]

## To develop in us a loving knowledge of the Son

The *Catechism* serves this single goal, then: that the Word, received in us through faith, might grow and mature until Christ is fully formed in each one of us.[9] The *Catechism* seeks to deepen the growth of the Word in the lives of Christians through developing the "loving knowledge"[10] of Christ in its readers.

This growth and formation of Christ in our lives clearly requires, in the first place, a *deepening of our understanding*. We need to grasp the overall shape and character of the faith, as well as to know the details of what the Good News entails for our lives. The *Catechism* provides us with what we need here, through its authoritative and definitive account of the Christian faith,[11] enabling each of us to have a mind made new in Christ, with a transformed outlook and new vision of things that comes from sharing in his life.[12] The *Catechism* sets before us a whole worldview, one that allows us to exercise a discernment of cultural and social currents within a rapidly-moving contemporary society, so as to be able to evaluate these in the light of the perennial, unchanging teachings of the Church.

## To provide for us an integrated formation by the Holy Spirit

The formation of our minds does not occur in isolation from the other aspects of our lives; and so the *Catechism* provides us with what we need for a *comprehensive and integrated formation* so that we can be conformed to Christ not only in our thoughts, but also in our words and actions.[13]

> "Great is the mystery of the faith!"...This mystery...
> requires that the faithful *believe* in it, that they *celebrate*
> it, and that they *live* from it in a vital and *personal
> relationship* with the living and true God.[14]

This formation comes about especially through the
action of the Holy Spirit in our lives, the one whom
the *Catechism* describes as "the interior Master of life
according to Christ, a gentle guest and friend who
inspires, guides, corrects and strengthens this life."[15]
When Mary asked, "How can this be?" the angel Gabriel
responded, "The Holy Spirit will come upon you." The
Holy Spirit is at the centre of this formation and our
relationship with him is fostered especially through
personal prayer. In the loving dialogue of prayer and
through the graces that flow from the sacred liturgy of
the Church, the *Catechism* speaks of the Son and the
Holy Spirit, the two "hands" of the Father,[16] being at
work for our transformation. The graces lavished upon
us in liturgy and prayer come to fruition, with our co-
operation, in the actions and decisions - both small and
large - we take, in our daily lives.

## To form us as disciples of Jesus Christ

This is another arena of formation, one characterised
by "a struggle, and a dramatic one, between good and
evil, between light and darkness".[17] The *Catechism* was
written to form the whole Church as a community
of disciples of Christ who by his grace conquer in that

struggle. It serves that great commission that Christ gave to his apostles after his resurrection to "make disciples of all nations".[18] This making of disciples is carried out especially through teaching and through the graces that flow from the sacraments. The *Catechism* therefore communicates the teachings of Christ in his Church and also alerts and educates us as to the presence and action of the Holy Spirit in the liturgy and in the heart as he awakens in us a desire to respond more and more deeply to the outpouring of God's grace and love for us.

The *Catechism* also offers us, as members of Christ's Body and sharers in his life, authoritative guidance for the Christian life, to "sustain hope in the midst of tribulations"[19] by shedding light on the actions and attitudes that characterise a truly blessed life, the life of the baptised.

## To prepare us to speak in the Name of Christ and his Church

The *Catechism* has been written to support the Church's mission of evangelisation. Christ is *the* Teacher in his Church, and he graciously offers us the opportunity to teach in his name.[20] The *Catechism* quotes from St Thomas Aquinas: "To teach in order to lead to faith is the task of every preacher and of each believer".[21] Teaching, we note, is the task of *every* disciple, every member of the People of God. The *Catechism* invites us *all* to share in this responsibility for teaching and for handing on what

11

we have received.[22] The *Catechism*'s genre is therefore precisely that of a teaching document.

The *Catechism* has been written, in other words, in order to help form the Christian community as a catechetical body, so that, having been enriched with the wisdom of God's revelation,[23] we can carry Christ to others. We can turn to Mary, Mother of the Church, to accompany us as we take up this challenge. The *Catechism* notes that, even while he was still in her womb, Mary carried the growing Christ to her cousin Elizabeth.[24] Mary's action here perfectly captures the unstoppable need of the true believer and disciple to witness to Christ.[25] Just as the Holy Spirit's work in the Blessed Virgin provides us with the model and pattern we follow in our receiving of the Word in our lives, so also her co-operation with the Holy Spirit is the paradigm for *every act of transmission* of this same Word to others.[26]

The *Catechism* speaks beautifully of the way in which we move from a knowledge of the divine Son to this work of teaching in his name: "From this loving knowledge of Christ springs the desire to proclaim him, to 'evangelise', and to lead others to the 'yes' of faith in Jesus Christ."[27] The *Catechism* also points to the reverse dynamic contained in mission: that our sharing increases in us the desire to know and love Christ better ourselves: "the need to know the faith better makes itself felt".

## To prompt us to ponder with Mary, the Mother of God

The Apostolic Letter introducing the *Catechism*, *Fidei Depositum,* speaks of this dual movement of ongoing *formation* and *mission* by presenting the Christ-child under the image of a "deposit", a scriptural image evoking the incalculable wealth that is given to us in Christ.[28] This divine Child is the true wealth of the Church; her riches lie wholly in him. Mary receives this, the wealth of the nations, into her womb. The opening sentence of this Apostolic Letter *Fidei Depositum*, "The Deposit of Faith", helps us to grasp the essential nature of the *Catechism* in a striking way: "Guarding the deposit of the faith is the mission entrusted to the Church and which she fulfils in every age". The two terms, "guarding" and "mission" are interdependent; each relies on the other.

The Blessed Virgin helps us to understand how this is the case. In the Gospel of St Luke, Mary is presented as holding together in her heart all that she is learning of her divine Son: "Mary kept all these things, pondering them in her heart".[29] The Greek word that is translated as "pondering" here is *symballousa*, a word connected to that which the Church was to come to use for the Creed, which is called a *symbolon* or "Symbol".[30] As the Mother of God, Mary ponders in her heart what she knows of Christ. He is the treasure of her soul. St Ambrose speaks of the Creed, the Symbol, centred as it is upon Christ, in a comparable way: the Creed, he says "is the spiritual seal, our heart's meditation and an ever-present guardian; it is, unquestionably, the treasure of our soul".[31]

The *Catechism* helps us to appreciate, then, the importance of Mary's ongoing meditation on the mysteries of Jesus, the Son of God and her Son, as a model for the reception and growth of Jesus Christ in our own lives.[32] The *Catechism* is a unique text for practising this continual prayerful reflection. At the same time, through this juxtaposing of guarding and mission the *Catechism* also encourages every member of Christ's Body to follow Mary's example in seeking to hand him on to others - bishops in the first place, as successors of the apostles, and also parents in the home, priests, deacons and catechists in parishes, teachers in educational institutions; each and every believer in the unique setting in which God has placed them.

We will see in the coming chapters that the content of the faith, centred on the person of Jesus Christ, is presented in the *Catechism* through a number of pedagogical principles[33] that make for a faithful and effective transmission of the faith. In this way the *Catechism* helps us all to co-operate fruitfully with the Holy Spirit, bearing Christ to the world that is in such need of the happiness he came to give.

## Consolidation exercise

▶ Read the whole Letter, *Fidei Depositum,* which Pope St John Paul II has written to you! It is quite short and you will find it directly following the *Contents* pages of the *Catechism.*

▶ As you read this Letter, look out for every reference indicating that this Letter and this *Catechism* is for everyone. It is most certainly for the bishops and priests, the key teachers, but it is also for the whole people of God. Begin at the very top: *"To my venerable Brothers... and to all the People of God".*

▶ Continue to look out for these and similar phrases, such as "People of God", "entire Church", "all the Lord Jesus's disciples", "Christian faithful", "all the faithful who wish to deepen their knowledge of the unfathomable riches of salvation".

▶ As you read you will notice that the *Catechism* has not been written only for Catholics. It is for all Christians, all the baptised. In fact, it is for all who are called to know Christ and receive his healing work in their lives - that is, every human being! You will see that John Paul refers to "every individual who asks us to give an account of the hope that is in us and who wants to know what the Catholic Church believes". Many people have found full communion in the Catholic Church after reading of the breadth, depth and beauty of the Christian faith in these pages of the *Catechism of the Catholic Church.*

# 2

# THE STRUCTURE:
## Four Dimensions of the Christian Life

From a consideration of the central purpose of the *Catechism* as an annunciation of the mysteries of the faith we now turn to examine its structure, how it is ordered and laid out for us. This might seem to be an inconsequential point, almost as though any structure or ordering would serve us as well as any other. We know the importance of accuracy in the presentation of the content of the truths of the faith; this point is probably so obvious that even to say it feels a little strange, like stating that recipes in cookbooks should be careful in how they list the ingredients. But the organising of how the recipes appear in the cookbook would seem to be less important, even though we obviously look for *some* kind of order simply for the sake of the easy use of the book.

In the case of the *Catechism*, though, the authors would like us to learn a good deal about the Christian faith precisely from this point about how the mysteries of the faith are organised for us here. Moreover, the *Catechism* might surprise us in the image it chooses to describe this structure. It asks us to consider its contents as a "melodious symphony of the truth".[34] God's revelation is compared to a symphony.

## To attract us to heavenly truth

This image of a symphony is used because it can help us to understand a number of important points about the *Catechism*. In the first place it reminds us that the faith, precisely because it is the ultimate truth, is intrinsically attractive. Symphonies are composed for their audiences, to inspire us, bring satisfaction, move us, speak to us of happiness, and to draw out and express the depths and the drama of human existence. When music is written to accompany events or dramatic scenes it can enhance and draw us closer to what is taking place. A powerful film score, for example, can transform our watching of a scene as it accompanies the action, communicating and commenting upon the events, providing through thematic phrases interpretative keys to what is taking place.

The Catholic faith is music played from *heaven*.[35] God is the composer of this symphony. And it is written to reflect and express the perfect happiness of his kingdom, our true home. When we focus on the spiritual beauty of the truths of the faith with this musical image in mind, we are reminded that they are addressed to the deepest desires of the heart, and that we are made for these divine truths, to find our completion and satisfaction in them. The *Catechism* asks us to think of its contents in the way St Augustine did when he approached the faith: "How is it, then, that I seek you, Lord? Since in seeking you, my God, I seek a happy life, let me seek you so that my soul may live, for my body draws life from my soul and my soul draws life from you".[36]

## To introduce us to the four dimensions of the Christian life

The image of a symphony can also help us to understand and appreciate the importance of the structure of the *Catechism*. A classical symphony usually has four movements. If you look at the contents pages you will see that the *Catechism* has four parts to it. We can think of these parts, then, as analogous to the movements found in a symphony by Haydn, Mozart or Beethoven.

The notion of the presentation of the Christian faith being made according to a fourfold pattern is deeply embedded in the Church's tradition. This same structure, for example, was also used for the *Roman Catechism* (1566), the universal catechism that was published following the Council of Trent and which influenced the education and formation of millions of Catholics through the local catechisms it inspired.[37]

In fact, this structure reaches right back to scriptural roots, to the *Acts of the Apostles* where there is a short passage describing the life of the Christians who lived in the earliest period of the Church. Of those who were newly baptised, following St Peter's speech at Pentecost, St Luke writes, "And they devoted themselves to the apostles' teaching and fellowship, to the breaking of bread and the prayers."[38] The four parts in the *Catechism* map onto these four features of early Christian life: the apostles' teaching (Part One), the breaking of bread (Part Two), fellowship (Part Three), and the prayers (Part four). The four elements making up the Catholic faith today are the same four that have always been present in the Church's life. The *Catechism* faithfully reiterates these same features that the apostles provided for the Church's life and growth. We can think of these as the four dimensions of the Christian life of each of us as we follow the path of discipleship.

The transmission of the faith also involves handing over the faith precisely in this fourfold way if it is to be undertaken fruitfully:

> Those who with God's help have welcomed Christ's call and freely responded to it are urged on by love of Christ to proclaim the Good News everywhere in the world. This treasure, received from the apostles, has been faithfully guarded by their successors. All Christ's faithful are called to hand it on from generation to generation, by *professing the faith*, by *living it in fraternal sharing*, and by celebrating it in *liturgy* and *prayer*.[39]

## To present a comprehensive overview of God's saving truths

The *Catechism* provides us with a comprehensive account of the essentials of the faith.[40] It is interesting that our word "comprehend" is related to the notion of being "comprehensive": we understand when we have a complete account of something. This is what the *Catechism* offers us.

A symphony, similarly, can only be appreciated when we hear it as a whole, when we listen to all of the movements. The *Catechism* is inviting us, then, through the use of this musical image, to the thought that a deep love for the faith is inseparable from our embrace of it *as a whole*. Each of the four "movements" needs to be followed, the four parts "heard", so that the unified presentation of the whole truth of the faith is grasped. Attempts to isolate portions of the faith from this unity, to separate them out, to single out particular aspects of the faith from the whole, are misconceived and lead to a growing indifference towards the faith. The glory of each aspect of the faith lies in part in the relation it bears to the whole symphony. The challenge for us as we study the *Catechism*, then, is to listen for this "whole" sounding its melody in the part we are reading,[41] not to shy away from the sections in minor keys, and even to learn to receive what seem like dissonances to our ears because of their contribution towards the beauty of the whole symphony.

Each part of the *Catechism* is presented in two sections. The *second section* of each part is called the "pillar" of that part.[42] We can recall that the Church is described in the New Testament as a building[43] and as the "pillar and bulwark of the truth".[44] Within these four dimensions that make up her life, four strong pillars stand out, supporting the whole. These pillars provide the complete, *comprehensive support* needed for the Christian life. These are the Creed (in the *Catechism*, Part One, Section Two), the Sacraments (Part Two, Section Two), the Commandments (Part Three, Section Two) and the Lord's Prayer (Part Four, Section Two). The second section of each part, then, is dedicated to introducing us to the pillar of that particular dimension, ensuring that our understanding of its importance is fully grasped.

The *first section* in each part of the *Catechism* provides us with the *foundations* on which the pillars are built. "If the foundations are destroyed", the psalmist asks, "what can the righteous do?".[45] The Church has called for a new evangelisation - an evangelisation of the People of God themselves - since so many of the foundational elements that are needed for the building of these pillars have been damaged by secularism and by the long-term neglect of serious adult formation in the faith. In each part we are offered in this first section the necessary elements for our understanding which will allow the pillars to be constructed strongly, as on rock.

## To support us in unifying truth and life

The four movements of a symphony, whilst distinct in terms of their tempo, key and individual character, are nonetheless united as elements of a single whole under a single key signature - the symphony is in C major, D minor, B flat major, or whatever. There is thus in any symphony an overall unity to the whole piece and the different movements both serve and express this unity. We have noted that truly to open oneself to the attractiveness and power of any particular symphony it is necessary to listen to it as a whole, to hear how the music flows from movement to movement. In the *Catechism*, the many truths - its many notes, harmonies and musical phrases - make up a single rich composition, a unity of Christian life and truth.

The uniting of the dimensions of truth and life is one of the special emphases of the *Catechism*. Ensuring the integrity of this relationship is the primary and ongoing challenge for all members of the Church in her task of mission, so that the witness of lives characterised by charity authentically reflect the deepest truths professed.

## To remind us of the primacy of grace

This unity of truth and life is possible only as a result of the unceasing work of God's saving grace. The ordering of the parts in the *Catechism* helps to remind us of this point. "The plan of the CCC [*Catechism of the Catholic Church*] is in itself a message".[46] It has been proposed that we see in this ordering of the parts a kind of diptych, with the first two parts of the *Catechism* making up one panel and parts three and four making up the second.

On the first panel we have the Creed's presentation of God, his nature and acts; we contemplate the awe-inspiring plan of God in creating, in redeeming that which was lost and in need of rescue, and in the work of sanctification. We then contemplate, in the *Catechism*'s second part, the ongoing *opus Dei*, the glorious "work of God" for our salvation that is communicated through the sacraments and liturgy of the Church. This panel is to be read first because God's work comes first. The primacy of this panel is also reflected in the fact that these two parts constitute two-thirds of the material in the *Catechism*.

On the second panel we contemplate the human response to the overwhelming goodness of God. We read first of what makes up our life in Christ under the tutelage and discipline of the Holy Spirit (Part Three) and then how the Holy Spirit enables us to be "in the presence of the thrice-holy God and in communion with him" in prayer (Part Four).[47]

Cardinal Schönborn explains this ordering as a constant reminder of the primacy of God's grace in the Christian life, a primacy that shapes our understanding of the faith and also how the Church explains and transmits this faith.[48]

## To hand on to us a sure reference point for the Catholic faith

It is precisely as a *unified, beautiful whole*, as a whole

symphony, that the Catholic faith carries conviction. The profession a person makes when he or she enters into full communion with the Catholic Church is to "believe and profess all that the holy Catholic Church believes, teaches, and proclaims to be revealed by God". The "all" here is one unified Truth. It is precisely in its capacity to express truth as a whole (and Catholic means "according to the whole")[49] that we are drawn to it and can find our security there and the reference point for our lives.

The human person craves meaning and cannot finally be satisfied with anything less than a meaning that *completely* satisfies, that can provide wisdom for the *whole* of life. For the human person "God alone satisfies", as St Thomas Aquinas said; nothing less than God can provide this. It is a point echoed by the sixteenth century Carmelite saint St Teresa of Jesus: "Whoever has God / wants for nothing / God alone is enough."[50] God alone is enough because he is the fulness of Being. He is the Source of all existence and so nothing that we seek is outside of his life.

Pope St John Paul II describes the *Catechism* as a "sure and authentic reference text" for teaching Catholic doctrine. He goes on to speak of its "showing carefully the content and wondrous harmony of the Catholic faith". Through his Church, Christ the Teacher offers us in the *Catechism* an account of the mysteries of the faith that is both comprehensive and coherent and that can therefore provide a secure reference point for us in every troubling situation and difficult question from the society around us. This is the sure reference point for forming our opinions rather than relying on the opinions of our neighbours or the media.

## Consolidation exercise

▶ Read *CCC* 13-17. These paragraphs summarise for you the basic structure, content and purpose of the entire text.

▶ Now that you have understood the structure of the *Catechism*, turn to the *Contents* pages and find for yourself the titles of the four parts and also of the two sections in each part.

# 3

## THE PRESENTATION:
### the Beautiful Way of Faith

We have seen that the *Catechism* has been written to catechise us, to provide a formation for us in all of the dimensions of the Christian life and to provide us with what we need to play our part in the transmission of the Christian faith.

This particular *Catechism* catechises through images as well as words. Even before opening the *Catechism*, the authors have already given us an image, a simple line drawing on the cover of the work, to sum up and express the most "characteristic aspects" of the *Catechism*.[51] Four works of art have then been placed within the pages of the *Catechism*, one piece to introduce each of the four parts.

Why is there this interest in using images, works of art, to teach the faith? The concise version of the *Catechism*, the *Compendium of the Catechism of the Catholic Church*, published in 2005, offers us a number of reasons.[52] Essentially it is because Jesus is both the *Image* of the unseen God and the *Word* of God;[53] and because Jesus is both the Image and the Word these two features of the *Catechism* work through a reciprocal illumination, with the images helping us to understand the words and the text in turn interpreting the images for us.

## To sum up the faith for us utterly simply

The *Catechism* appeals to us to grasp the truths of the Word of God through what we might call a "gaze of faith".[54] In particular it is intended that the logo on the front cover sum up and express for us the key features of the faith so as to provide an utterly simple overview of all that is contained in the pages of the *Catechism*. You will notice that the logo places the Good Shepherd at the centre, affirming that in the *Catechism* the reader will be discovering Christ as the heart of all that is presented,[55] and also that the truths that are placed before us are meant to lead us to "lie down in green pastures", as we see the sheep lying peacefully at the feet of the Shepherd. The sheep, as we have noted in the last chapter, is attentive to the Good Shepherd since it is listening to the symphony of truth, the beautiful melody being played. Eternal life is depicted in the overarching tree, in the shade of whose branches and fruit both sheep and Shepherd rest. The pastoral authority of the Shepherd, expressing the protective function of sacred doctrine, is expressed in the Shepherd's seated position[56] and staff.

## To reveal the unity of the dimensions of the faith

If the logo on the front cover sums up for us the whole of the *Catechism*, each of the four works of art beautifully encapsulate the central features of the four parts of the *Catechism* that they introduce.

• An image of the Blessed Virgin with Child, taken from a fresco of the third century, introduces the first part of the *Catechism*. We have seen that this image of the Virgin, fruitful with her divine Child, lies at the very heart, not only of the faith itself, but also of how we are to understand the transmission of the faith. The image includes a figure pointing to a star, reminding us of the prophecy from the time of the Old Covenant that "a star shall come out of Jacob",[57] a prophecy fulfilled in the birth of Christ. The image therefore places before us the whole of God's plan for our salvation coming to its peak in the birth of Christ. The Creed and all of the Church's doctrine revolves around this central truth.

• A fresco from the catacombs of Sts Marcellinus and Peter in Rome, dating from the fourth century, introduces the second part, on liturgy and the sacraments. The depiction of the woman with the haemorrhage touching the hem of Christ's garment communicates to us the crucial teaching of the Church that all that was visible in Christ is present in the sacraments of the Church so that it is here that we touch his Body today and from which his power goes out to heal us and bring us new life in him.

• A portrait of Christ on a sarcophagus dating from 359 sums up the third part, "life in Christ". This new life is depicted as a gift of two scrolls of the new law to Sts Peter and Paul. This new law is the grace of the Holy Spirit who enables us to live according to all that Christ taught for our benefit.[58]

• Finally, a miniature from the beginning of the second millennium, depicting the moment in the Gospels where the disciples, seeing Christ at prayer, ask him to teach them to pray, introduces the fourth part of the *Catechism*. The amazing nature of Christian prayer is shown, consisting in our sharing in the life and love of the Blessed Trinity, learning from God the Son how to pray to the Father in the Holy Spirit.

## To remind us of the rich Christian heritage of art

The Church has a "rich patrimony of Christian iconography"[59] - works of art form an essential part of the heritage of the faith that we can present when we hand on the faith. Placing some of these in the *Catechism* reminds us to pay due regard to this aspect of the Church's heritage and to appreciate the tremendous riches of the Christian tradition that is enshrined in its art. There are distinctive traditions of art in both the Eastern and Western branches of the Church, as well as many individual local cultural styles. The art works take many forms - stained glass, fresco, illuminated pages, icons, statues, wood-carvings, architectural features in glass and stone, and so on. This patrimony is a precious one and the *Catechism* emphasises that "bishops, personally or through delegates, should see to the promotion of sacred art, old and new, in all its forms".[60] The four art works used in the *Catechism* introduce us to this patrimony of both East and West, and to works spanning both the first and second millennia of the Christian Tradition.

## To show us the Word made flesh

This patrimony exists because the Divine Word assumed our flesh. The New Testament speaks powerfully of this: "That which was from the beginning, which we have heard, which we have seen with our eyes, which we have looked at and our hands have touched - this we proclaim".[61] God took human nature to himself and revealed himself through this nature.

Something more than words, therefore, is needed to convey the faith.[62] The coming among us in the flesh of God the Son is a coming that has "ushered in a new 'economy' of images".[63] The *Catechism* cites St John Damascene, one of the great defenders of Christian iconography: "now that he has made himself visible in the flesh and has lived with men, I can make an image of what I have seen of God…and contemplate the glory of the Lord, his face unveiled".[64]

The presence of these works of art in the *Catechism* can remind us, then, of something essential about the faith: that God appeared in visible form, so that his Face could be seen and contemplated, that we could see the healing gaze of his love.

## To manifest for us the glory of the Word in the created world

The creation itself is a manifestation of God's glory, luminous with his presence, and the history of salvation recalls numerous other events that are epiphanies of the divine -

> For Christ plays in ten thousand places,
> Lovely in limbs, and lovely in eyes not his
> To the Father through the features of men's faces.[65]

The *Catechism*'s value as a book lies in part in its ability to open our eyes to other "books" in which Christ the divine Word and presence appears to us - the "book" of nature, the "book" of the sacraments, the "book" of all who bear the divine image and likeness and who live around us, the "book of history" and the events of daily life - all that the *Catechism* calls "the page on which the 'today' of God is written".[66] The *Catechism* is not a text that closes us in on itself; it is rather one that has been given to us to be an avenue into the manifestations of God that are around us at each moment, to help us to reach into every place where the Lord's beauty is present and made real to us, where he can be seen, heard and touched. The *Catechism* wishes to open up to us and to express what has been called the "*via pulchritudinis*",[67] the way of beauty.

## To present the mysteries with effectiveness and lyricism

Works of art can teach us the mysteries of the faith. The five art pieces in the *Catechism* (and the further fourteen in the *Compendium*) are intended not only to beautify the text and make it more attractive, but to offer "the principal facts of the mystery of salvation to the contemplation and wonder of believers by presenting them in the splendour of colour and in the perfection of beauty".[68] Colours can highlight the splendour of the divine realm and the work of grace, and so the Christian artistic traditions typically include colour schemes that represent certain features of creation and of the faith (we can think of the liturgical colours, for example, following the seasons of the Church's year, or the common use of gold to signify divinity). The goodness and truth of the faith are expressed artistically through clarity and proportion and are grasped through this attractive medium.

Works of art manifest the "mystery of salvation" in a particular way. In a picture, the whole of the subject matter can be presented for the gaze of the viewer so that this "whole" can be grasped single and entire. The *Catechism* speaks often of the powerful impact that a "harmony" of signs makes to the way in which faith is conveyed since this speaks directly to the harmony for which every human person longs and seeks to recover since its loss at the beginning of time.[69] In great works of art the unity of the subject matter can be strongly brought out and there is a coherence to the presentation through the arrangement and depiction of the matter, so that the wholeness and integrity of the faith becomes visible.

Having learned from these works we can use them to hand on the faith to others: "today more than ever, in a culture of images, a sacred image can express much more than what can be said in words, and be an extremely effective and dynamic way of communicating the Gospel message".[70] Pope Pius XII reminds us that

> artistic masterpieces were known as the "Bible of the people", to mention such noted examples as the windows of Chartres, the door of Ghiberti (by happy expression known as the Door of Paradise), the Roman and Ravenna mosaics and the facade of the Cathedral of Orvieto. These and other masterpieces not only translate into easy reading and universal language the Christian truths, they also communicate the intimate sense and emotion of these truths with an effectiveness, lyricism and ardour that, perhaps, is not contained in even the most fervent preaching.[71]

In his call to evangelisation, Pope Francis reaffirms the importance of the *via pulchritudinis* in our transmission of the faith: "If, as St Augustine says, we love only that which is beautiful,[72] the incarnate Son, as the revelation of infinite beauty, is supremely lovable and draws us to himself with bonds of love. So a formation in the *via pulchritudinis* ought to be part of our effort to pass on the faith."[73] The *Catechism* offers just such a formation.

## *Consolidation exercise*

▶ Take time to look attentively at the logo on the front cover of the *Catechism* and identify all of the features of the Christian message you can find there.

▶ Then read what the *Catechism* itself says about this logo. You will find this explanation on the page with the publication details, just before the *Contents* pages. Show someone what you have discovered and introduce the *Catechism* to them using this logo.

▶ Finally, find the four works of art and read the *Catechism* text on the back of each picture.

# 4

## THE CENTRE:
## a Faith about Persons

The single feature of the *Catechism* that first strikes most people is its size. The *Catechism* is an immense work. This is as it should be, for its subject matter is immense: the infinite God. We think of the cosmos as vast, but Julian of Norwich, an English mystic who lived in the Middle Ages, was granted a vision of the whole of creation as "something small, no bigger than a hazelnut, lying in the palm of my hand".[74] For the Lord, the islands are like fine dust, mused Isaiah, the nations like drops of water in a bucket.[75]

The Christian tradition is deeply aware of the awe with which we must approach God and his revelation. The *Catechism* reminds us that God dwells in unapproachable light, and yet has chosen to make himself known to the creatures he has made. He has done so in order that they might share in his life of inexpressible joy.[76] Yet, inexplicably, the human person, created in God's own image and formed in his likeness, chose to reject the very purpose underlying his own creation, turn his back on perfect Love, and pursue a quest for satisfaction outside of Reality itself.

God's unceasing pursuit of his creatures even in their flight, taking on their fallen condition and eventually suffering and dying at their hands, only to rise again for the sake of their healing and redemption: this is the centre of the drama told so powerfully in the *Catechism*.

The *Catechism* is an immense volume because its central subject is the infinite God. In addition it provides us with the overarching account of the whole of creation, from its beginning to its consummation. As well as being an immense work, it is also a detailed and precise text since it is concerned to trace with care and attention the paths by which Christ and the Holy Spirit, the two "hands" of the eternal Father,[77] now offer the grace and guidance for each and every person to follow on the way of redemption, following the rescue of the human race from the power of darkness.[78]

"Salvation history" is the name tradition has given to the precious account of our rescue, and an account of this history provides the structure for many of the sections in the *Catechism*. The Church's dogmas themselves are presented in the *Catechism* as "lights along the path of faith" which "illuminate it and make it secure".[79] The truths of the faith, then, are only rightly understood when appreciated as "saving truths",[80] and the importance of the Church's whole mission is grasped correctly only when seen as "salvific".[81]

We can too easily think of the Church's teachings as dry and abstract. But all of the content in the *Catechism* is rightly perceived once we realise that it is centred upon persons - the divine Persons of the Blessed Trinity, and created personal beings, angelic and human. To provide us with this understanding, the *Catechism* has drawn together three scriptural verses to serve as the entry point into the text:

> FATHER, ...this is eternal life, that they may know you, the only true God, and Jesus Christ whom you have sent.

> God our Saviour desires all men to be saved and to come to the knowledge of the truth.

> There is no other name under heaven given among men by which we must be saved - than the name of JESUS.[82]

The quotations remind us of two things: first, that the whole of the content of the *Catechism* is given to us for the sake of salvation; and secondly, that knowledge of the truths found here is not impersonal but leads us into a personal knowing of the Father. This is made possible only through Jesus, the Incarnate Word, the one who is "in the bosom of the Father" and has made him known.[83] Dogmas are personal realities. The whole of doctrine is gathered together around the Person of Jesus.

## To introduce us to the Holy Trinity

The living centre of the Christian faith is the three Persons of the One God, God the Blessed Trinity. For this reason the most essential and fundamental section of the whole *Catechism* is that which presents God to us.[84] This is what the *Catechism* teaches:

> The mystery of the Most Holy Trinity is the central mystery of Christian faith and life. It is the mystery of God in himself. It is therefore the source of all the other mysteries of faith, the light that enlightens them.[85]

This statement makes clear that the teaching we find on the Blessed Trinity cannot simply be read and then put to one side. This mystery of God himself is the light that allows us to see and understand all of the other elements of the faith. The *Catechism* treats this very seriously, ensuring that every "mystery"[86] of Christian faith and life - that is, every Christian belief to which we hold and every aspect of our lives as Christians - is shown to flow from the divine Persons.[87] The *Catechism* helps us to appreciate that the Christian life is really a life of relationship with the Persons of the Trinity; it is our life with the Father who sees in secret, with the Son who has united us to himself through his taking flesh and becoming our brother, and with the Holy Spirit who at every moment is present to our inmost being to teach and heal us and prompt us how to act.[88] Prayer, also, is simply the "habit of being in the presence of the thrice-holy God and in communion with him".[89] As we read any section of the *Catechism*, we should look especially for the structuring presence of the Blessed Trinity.

## To make clear God's plan of sheer goodness

The Trinitarian underpinning of every doctrine and part of life appears in the pages of the *Catechism* mainly through its presentation of God's plan of loving goodness, his plan of salvation.[90] In this plan, one "formed from all eternity in Christ", the Father sends "his beloved Son, our Lord Jesus Christ, and the Holy Spirit" to lead us into the life of his own blessedness. The very first paragraph of the *Catechism* presents this plan in summary form, and this then appears as the great recurring theme flowing through the whole of the text:

> God, infinitely perfect and blessed in himself, in a plan of sheer goodness freely created man to make him share in his own blessed life. For this reason, at every time and in every place, God draws close to man. He calls man to seek him, to know him, to love him with all his strength. He calls together all men, scattered and divided by sin, into the unity of his family, the Church. To accomplish this, when the fulness of time had come, God sent his Son as Redeemer and Saviour. In his Son and through him, he invites men to become, in the Holy Spirit, his adopted children and thus heirs of his blessed life.[91]

The name given by the Church for such a summary articulation of God's plan, so exquisitely presented here in this opening paragraph, is the "initial proclamation of the Gospel", and the whole of the Church's catechesis is founded upon it.[92] It is a plan that develops in stages, across the centuries, from the moment of creation.[93] Often the plan is called "the economy of salvation",[94] and in the *Catechism* the plan is sometimes described as consisting of three great "periods", corresponding to the revelation of the Persons to us: before Christ's coming there is the time of the Old Covenant, the time when the Father was revealed and the period of the promises relating to Jesus's appearing; the second period is that of the New Covenant, the fulfilment of the promises, the time when the Son is revealed; finally, the age of the Church is the final age of the world, the period when the Spirit is revealed, and the time of the sacramental economy. The culmination of the plan is, of course, the return of Christ, the Bridegroom, the final judgement and the coming of God's Kingdom in its fulness.

## To illuminate God's plan that carries every moment of faith and life

God wants us to know our true identity by finding ourselves in his plan, by knowing that this is where we belong. The opening paragraph of the *Catechism*'s part on the Christian life is a clarion call to us to do this:

Christian, recognise your dignity and, now that you share in God's own nature, do not return to your former base condition by sinning. Remember who is your head and of whose body you are a member. Never forget that you have been rescued from the power of darkness and brought into the light of the Kingdom of God.[95]

We recognise who we are once we see ourselves from the point of view of God's plan. Then we know our true face: we share in God's own nature. Our true home is God's kingdom of light, now that we have been rescued from the power of darkness. This statement is placed at the very opening of the part since it is upon such a fundamental recognition that our desire for the Christian life grows.

The Creed itself, in Part One of the *Catechism*, is of course a profession of faith concerning this plan of God's goodness. The Creed is structured in three parts, and the *Catechism* presents it for us in three chapters, one focused on each of the Persons. In this way, every teaching in the first part of the *Catechism* is located within this "plan of sheer goodness".[96]

The liturgy and sacraments, and the life of prayer, are also positioned within God's plan. We understand the place of each sacrament in the life of the Church when we appreciate its unique place in the Father's loving plan. The opening paragraph in Part Two focuses our attention on this point:

In the Symbol of the faith the Church confesses the mystery of the Holy Trinity and of the plan of God's "good pleasure" for all creation: the Father accomplishes the "mystery of his will" by giving his beloved Son and his Holy Spirit for the salvation of the world and for the glory of his name. Such is the mystery of Christ, revealed and fulfilled in history according to the wisely ordered plan that St Paul calls the "plan of the mystery" and the patristic tradition will call the "economy of the Word incarnate" or the "economy of salvation".[97]

We are reminded that our worship and our participation in the sacraments is part of the ordered plan of God for our redemption. The *Catechism*'s treatment of prayer, also, is placed within the three "eras" of God's "wisely ordered plan", a plan of sheer goodness.[98]

### To invite us to converse with God

The *Catechism* emphasises that God's plan is to bring us into his communion of perfect love:

By sending his only Son and the Spirit of Love in the fulness of time, God has revealed his innermost secret: God himself is an eternal exchange of love, Father, Son and Holy Spirit, and he has destined us to share in that exchange.[99]

Heaven is to live with the Holy Trinity, with the angels and all the blessed in a state of complete happiness; and such a life of communion, the *Catechism* teaches, can begin even

44

now, on earth. In the opening paragraphs of its first part the *Catechism* reminds us of this purpose of human life, to live in everlasting communion with the God of love and with all those who share in this love: "this invitation to converse with God is addressed to man *as soon as he comes into being*".[100] Communion with God and with others is defined as the very heart of what it means to exist:

> For if man exists it is because God has created him through love, and through love continues to hold him in existence. He cannot live fully according to truth unless he freely acknowledges that love and entrusts himself to his creator.[101]

Prayer is the result of such an acknowledgement and is our entry into this life of communion. It is "the life of the new heart"; through prayer we remain in communion with "him who is our life and our all".[102] So that our heart can be in tune with the Heart of Christ the simple invocation of the name of Jesus is recommended as "the simplest way of praying always",[103] and such repetition reminds us that prayer is "communion with Christ and extends throughout the Church, which is his Body. Its dimensions are those of Christ's love."[104]

## To save us from an endless disintegration

We have already met the *Catechism*'s teaching that the human person is "divided in himself" and that, as a result, "the whole life of men, both individual and social, shows itself to be a struggle, and a dramatic one".[105] In seeking our salvation, God seeks to make us whole and to heal us of divisions, both internally and with one another. The Holy Spirit accomplishes this work in us by "mobilising the whole being", spirit, will, feelings, intellect and affections.[106] He seeks to renew us interiorly so that we are transformed and made new.[107] The authors of the *Catechism* are deeply concerned that the *Catechism* should serve this central human and Christian task of integration. Only in relation to God is this integration made possible:

> Human life finds its unity in the adoration of the one God. The commandment to worship the Lord alone integrates man and saves him from an endless disintegration.[108]

The whole of the *Catechism* serves this overarching purpose. So that our experience of learning about the faith should draw us more and more deeply and securely into the path of salvation, the *Catechism* has been planned as an integrated, "organic" learning of the faith. "This catechism is conceived as an *organic presentation* of the Catholic faith in its entirety. It should be seen therefore as a unified whole."[109] By "organic" the *Catechism* means that our learning of the faith is a learning, from beginning to end, about the ways, the plans and the nature of *the living God*. "Organic" reminds us that "he is the living God who wants men to live".[110]

The *Catechism* has been prepared, therefore, as an organic text in order to bring us to life in God. Our learning of the faith can be thought of as analogous to our learning about any living thing. When we encounter a living organism we do not relate to it primarily in terms of "parts"; rather, we encounter a whole being. On meeting a person and shaking their hand, for example, I do not speak of having met a hand, but a person. When I meet a doctrine I meet the Lord, his saving nature and plan.

To enable us to learn the faith as a living unity, and to bring *us* into a living unity in Christ, the *Catechism* has included the unusual feature of cross-references, placed alongside the paragraphs.[111] These references are carefully positioned to take us to other parts of the *Catechism*. They serve a number of related purposes, with the additional paragraphs sometimes developing a point or expanding it, sometimes helping to define a term, but most of all ensuring that, through our following up these references, the four dimensions of the faith - and of our lives - are continually being united.

## To gather us into one by the love of Christ

The plan of God, moreover, is not just to heal us as individuals. Rather, it is to unite and bring into communion *with one another* all those made in his image and likeness. God did not create us to be solitary beings, alone and isolated, and he does not save us alone. Where sin has brought division, the love of Christ gathers and reconciles.

The *Catechism* draws our attention to the Church's tradition which uses the phrase *Christus totus* - "the whole Christ" - to describe the outcome of this gathering.[112] The whole Christ is Christ the Head with all of the members of his Body.

To reunite all his children, scattered and led astray by sin, the Father willed to call the whole of humanity together into his Son's Church. The Church is the place where humanity must rediscover its unity and salvation.[113]

God wills to save us in the one Church, as members of the one Person, Jesus Christ. We are each of us made in the image of a Trinitarian God, made for a life of mutual exchange that will find its completion and fulness in sharing in the life of the Blessed Trinity themselves.[114]

## Consolidation exercise

▶ It would be good to undertake a short "organic reading".

▶ Read *CCC* 368. This paragraph explains the meaning of the term "heart" when applied to the human person.

▶ You will see that there are side references that take you into all four parts of the *Catechism*. These help us to contemplate the place of the human heart in each of the dimensions of the Christian life. Read the following four references:

▶ *CCC* 478: Part One: this teaches us about Christ's human heart

▶ *CCC* 1431: Part Two: this examines the conversion of the heart in the Sacrament of Reconciliation

▶ *CCC* 2517: Part Three: this reference takes us to the ninth commandment and the purification of the heart in daily life

▶ *CCC* 2562: Part Four: the heart is identified as the locus for prayer

# 5

# THE LIVING SOURCES:
## Holy Scripture and Sacred Tradition

As we read through the paragraphs in any topic area we will be struck by the extent to which they draw in the Scriptures and sources from the Church's Tradition. The *Catechism*'s preference is to use citations from the Holy Scriptures, the liturgy, and the Fathers of the Church wherever possible, allowing these sources of the faith to speak directly to us.[115] In *Fidei Depositum*, Pope St John Paul speaks of his desire that catechesis be renewed at what he calls the "living sources of the faith". The language of the *Catechism* therefore deliberately grounds us in these "living sources", helping us at every moment into the vocabulary and terminology which carries God's revelation. So important is this point that an extensive index of these sources is part of the official, definitive text of the *Catechism*.

## To soak us in Scripture, the word of God

A glance at the foot of any page of the *Catechism* indicates the overriding importance of the Scriptures, both the Old and the New Testaments, in the compilation of the *Catechism*, and this initial impression is confirmed on a closer inspection of the index of sources itself. Every book of the New Testament is represented as well as almost every book of the Old Testament.[116] The text is "soaked"[117] in Scripture from beginning to end. Cardinal Ratzinger, who oversaw the development of the *Catechism*, wrote that, "As far as I know, there has never been until now a catechism so thoroughly formed by the Bible".[118]

The *Catechism* provides us with forty paragraphs of invaluable teaching on the principles for a Catholic reading of the Scriptures and naturally it uses these same principles in the text itself.[119] This section repays close attention and several points may be made here:

• The *Old Testament* witnesses in a hidden way to the mystery of our salvation, to "the whole divine pedagogy of God's saving love".[120] This hiddenness is brought into the light when Christ appears and he is the key for interpreting the entire period of the "promises" which point towards him.[121]

• The *Gospels* are the heart of the Scriptures "because they are the principal source for the life and teaching of the Incarnate word, our Saviour".[122] In the face of widespread scepticism, and without naivety, the *Catechism* unhesitatingly affirms the historicity of the Gospels and confirms that they "have told us the honest truth about Jesus".[123] In its treatment of the Virgin Birth, the miracles of Jesus, and Christ's bodily resurrection, for example, the *Catechism*'s text clearly and unambiguously confirms the historicity of these events.[124]

• There is a *spiritual sense* to the Scriptures as well as a literal sense, since God is the author of the Scriptures, and he inspired the human authors. The Scriptures communicate to us, and reflect upon, God's unified, saving plan of love. Because of the unity of this plan, the realities and events upon which the text comments, as well as the text itself, can be signs of other things. The "spiritual sense" of the Scriptures does not refer, then, to something rarefied or unearthly; on the contrary, it is the conviction that the meaning of the text and of those realities in the "economy of salvation" are not bounded and contained but that, belonging to God's plan, they reach into every part of history and of our lives. In particular they can refer to Christ - the historical Christ and also *Christus totus*, Christ as Head and members (this is called the "allegorical" meaning), they can provide guidance for our life in Christ (the "moral" meaning), and they can also point us towards our heavenly fulfilment still to come (the "anagogical" meaning). The Church reads the Scriptures with these meanings in mind and the teachings in the different parts of the *Catechism* are informed by them: the allegorical meaning in the first part of the *Catechism*, the moral meaning in the third part of the *Catechism*, and the anagogical meaning in the second and fourth parts of the *Catechism*. In this way the whole of the *Catechism* can be considered as both a literal and a spiritual reading of the Scriptures.[125]

## To enable our growth through the obedience of faith

The Scriptures have a place of authority in the Church because God is their author. "Author" and "authority" can both be traced back to the same Latin word, *auctor*, which signifies a point of origination and also that of increase and the giving of growth. An author is both the source of a text and the one who provides for the growth and development of the text. St John Paul II wanted the Church to renew herself at the "living sources of the faith" since these provide for growth in the Christian life. When we allow these sources from Scripture and Tradition to be authoritative for us, we are placing ourselves where we can receive God's blessing, from the Source of all growth and fruitfulness. We are allowing God to be a Father to us, providing for us all that we need in Christ, lavishing upon us "every spiritual blessing in the heavenly places".[126]

The proper response to God's authority, meeting us in Holy Scripture and Sacred Tradition, is an act of trust in what we read and obedience with regard to it; this is called the "obedience of faith".[127] It happens by grace when we, with the Blessed Virgin Mary, say *fiat*, "Be it done to me". The *Catechism* teaches:

> By faith, man completely submits his intellect and his will to God. With his whole being man gives his assent to God the revealer. Sacred Scripture calls this

human response to God, the author of revelation, "the obedience of faith".[128]

It offers us two models of such obedience, Abraham and Mary.[129] In both cases their obedience of faith is united to the promise of growth from God: Abraham was to be the Father of many nations; Mary becomes the Mother of the Redeemer, and then of all the disciples of her Son. Of Abraham, the *Catechism* writes, "Because he was 'strong in his faith', Abraham became the 'father of all who believe'",[130] while of the Blessed Virgin it teaches that she "most perfectly embodies the obedience of faith"[131]. Christ is conceived and grows and is born in her precisely because of her obedience, her *fiat*.

To teach timeless truths given in history

The *Catechism* has gathered together for us into one volume sources that carry God's timeless revelation to us. Because God is eternal, the truth he speaks, the revelation he gives, is not bound to a particular time, but can speak to all times.

This revelation was given in its fulness in the Person of the Son, the Word of God, who took our flesh. The *Catechism* quotes from St John of the Cross, underlining the completeness of this revelation:

> In giving us his Son, his only Word (for he possesses no other), he spoke everything to us at once in this sole Word - and he has no more to say...because

what he spoke before to the prophets in parts, he has now spoken all at once by giving us the All Who is His Son.[132]

At a particular point in history, human nature was united to the divine Person of the Son, the whole Mystery of God united to a particular body, place and time. In Christ, the eternal God spoke to us. God speaks *in time for all time*. As the *Catechism* explains,

> all that Christ is - all that he did and suffered for all men - participates in the divine eternity, and so transcends all times while being made present in them all.[133]

Through the last two thousand years of the life and mission of the Church, the living sources carrying this revelation (the Scriptures, the Councils of the Church, the liturgy, the Fathers and Doctors of the Church) have brought new life to every age and place. They bring this life to us by lifting us beyond our immediate experiences and the limitations of our particular time and connecting us to that wider stream, the experiences of the whole of the People of God in salvation history, and to the Mystery of Christ himself. It is the work of the Holy Spirit in the Church to bring us to this richer and wider life, giving us this "growth" through the sources, and so the *Catechism* describes the Holy Spirit as "the Church's living memory".[134]

## To provide access to the language of the faith

The *Catechism* honours the God-inspired speech made known to us in the sources that carry his revelation. The text of the *Catechism* stays as close as possible to the biblical terms and phrases that are an intrinsic part of the worldview of the Scriptures.

While this can present challenges for us at times, as modern readers facing a sometimes unfamiliar term or phrase, the *Catechism* in this way leads us to conform our ideas and views to those of revelation, rather than the other way around. St Paul wrote to the Christian community in Rome, "Do not be conformed to this world, but be transformed by the renewing of your minds".[135]

The maintaining and development of a living Christian culture depends upon this.

> The Church, "the pillar and bulwark of the truth", faithfully guards "the faith which was once for all delivered to the saints". She guards the memory of Christ's words; it is she who from generation to generation hands on the apostles' confession of faith. As a mother who teaches her children to speak and so to understand and communicate, the Church our Mother teaches us the language of faith in order to introduce us to the understanding and the life of faith.[136]

The Scriptures, traditions and practices in the biblical world, as we have seen, in turn informed the developing

Christian language and culture, and the Church encourages us stay as close as possible to these original terms and the language of the sources, both as a means of ensuring faithfulness to the content of the Church's teaching and also for the sake of helping to develop in ourselves a biblical, liturgical and ecclesial worldview. Through this adherence to the language of the sources the *Catechism* helps us to be formed ourselves in the precision and the "tone" of the inspired Scriptures, of the saints of the Church, and of her Fathers and Doctors.

## To bring us into the manifold co-operation of Mary and the saints

The *Catechism*'s index of sources reminds us of how God loves to involve his creatures in his work of redemption and sanctification. God is the First Cause of all that is. He loves to make use of secondary causes. This is a point the *Catechism* emphasises over and again. As the author of the Scriptures, for example, God inspired human authors, using their own faculties, to co-operate with him. Thus, "though he acted in them and by them, it was as true authors that they consigned to writing whatever he wanted written, and no more".[137] The liturgy is the work of Christ *and* his Church.[138] Prayer springs forth "from both the Holy Spirit *and* ourselves".[139] To carry out his providential plan God "makes use of his creatures' co-operation" so that they become fellow-workers in his Kingdom through their prayers, actions and sufferings.[140]

The pages of the *Catechism* are replete with quotations from the saints, and from the Fathers, Popes and Doctors of the Church. They remind us that it is as a Body, its members co-operating and supporting each other, that God's plan is enacted. The text draws attention to the special place that Mary has in this work, so that in heaven "by her manifold intercession" she continues to "bring us the gifts of eternal salvation".[141] Mary is the exemplary "type", or model, of the Church in this regard[142] and she helps us to understand the presence of that whole section of the sources that comes under the heading "Ecclesiastical Writers". The writings of these figures all contribute to that growth in the Church that comes about when members of the Body of Christ place themselves under authority, responding with an obedience of faith, thereby helping to "fix the whole Church more firmly in holiness".[143]

## To set us securely on the heavenward path

The sources have been gathered, then, to lead us to holiness, to the happiness of heaven. The *Catechism* presents this patchwork of sources, carefully compiled and arranged, for one purpose only: to provide for that increase and growth that leads to the salvation of all. From the line-drawing on the front cover, with the image of the Shepherd calling us to rest and guarding us by the authority of his staff, to the Scriptures culminating in the marriage of the Bride and the Lamb, to the voices of the saints, following the secure path by the guiding light of the dogmas of the Church, the selection of sources has this single overriding goal: to direct us to "the love that never ends".[144]

The path to heaven is followed through exercising the virtues of faith, hope and love. In one sense these virtues structure the whole of the *Catechism*: when we read the paragraphs in the Prologue which deal with the structure of the *Catechism* (*CCC* 13-17), we may have noted that the parts are each seen as related to one of the virtues. This is, in fact, a traditional structuring principle for catechisms. Part One is especially concerned with the virtue of faith, naturally enough; Part Three with the virtue of love, and Part Four with the virtue of hope. The second part of the *Catechism* is that in which all the virtues flow together, for it is in the sacraments and the liturgy that we find the profession of faith, the Lord's Prayer, directing us to hope, and the grace poured out to enable us to lead lives of love. The Eucharist, in fact, is called "the sum and summary of our faith". This is, above all, where the *Catechism* directs us to be fed, to receive the pledge of the life to come and to be filled with "every heavenly blessing and grace" to sustain us on that journey home to the Father's house.[145]

## *Consolidation exercise*

▶ Read the Gospel of Luke Chapter 1, or a chapter from any part of the New Testament.

▶ Then turn to the index of sources and find this chapter in the index and follow the *Catechism* references, reading those paragraphs. Notice which teachings of the Church in each part of the *Catechism*, each dimension of the Christian life, this scriptural chapter has informed.

# Sample *Catechism* Pages, Annotated.

Left-hand pages identify the title of the part of the *Catechism*

himself God, the Word made flesh: "No one has ever seen God; the only Son, who is in the bosom of the Father, he has made him known."[20] Because he "has seen the Father", Jesus Christ is the only one who knows him and can reveal him.[21]

The content is presented in numbered paragraphs for easy reference and reading

### To believe in the Holy Spirit

152. One cannot believe in Jesus Christ without sharing in his Spirit. It is the Holy Spirit who reveals to men who Jesus is. For "no one can say 'Jesus is Lord', except by the Holy Spirit,"[22] who "searches everything, even the depths of God.... No one comprehends the thoughts of God, except the Spirit of God."[23] Only God knows God completely: we believe *in* the Holy Spirit because he is God.

*The Church never ceases to proclaim her faith in one only God: Father, Son, and Holy Spirit.*

232

## III. The Characteristics of Faith

### Faith is a grace

153. When St Peter confessed that Jesus is the Christ, the Son of the living God, Jesus declared to him that this revelation did not come "from flesh and blood", but from "my Father who is in heaven."[24] *Faith is a gift of God, a supernatural virtue infused by him.* "Before this faith can be exercised, man must have the grace of God to move and assist him; he must have the interior helps of the Holy Spirit, who moves the heart and converts it to God, who opens the eyes of the mind and 'makes it easy for all to accept and believe the truth.'"[25]

Headings and sub-headings help us to see the main points and structure

### Faith is a human act

154. Believing is possible only by grace and the interior helps of the Holy Spirit. But it is no less true that believing is an authentically human act. Trusting in God and cleaving to the truths he has revealed are contrary neither to human freedom nor to human reason. Even in human relations it is not contrary to our dignity to believe what other persons tell us about themselves and their intentions or to trust their promises (for example, when a man and a woman marry) to share a communion of life with one another. If this is so, still less is it contrary to our dignity to "yield by faith the full

The text engages both mind and heart

20 *Jn* 1:18.
21 *Jn* 6:46; cf. *Mt* 11:27.
22 *1 Cor* 12:3.
23 *1 Cor* 2:10-11.
24 *Mt* 16:17; cf. *Gal* 1:15; *Mt* 11:29.
25 *DV* 5; cf. *DS* 377; 3010.

The living sources of the faith form the heart of the *Catechism*'s text submission of... intellect and will to God who reveals",[26] and to share in an interior communion with him.

155. In faith, the human intellect and will co-operate with divine grace: "Believing is an act of the intellect assenting to the divine truth by command of the will moved by God through grace."[27]    *20*

The *Catechism* explains *why* we believe as well as what we believe

#### Faith and understanding

156. What moves us to believe is not the fact that revealed truths appear as true and intelligible in the light of our natural reason: we believe "because of the authority of God himself who reveals them, who can neither deceive nor be deceived."[28] So "that the submission of our faith might nevertheless be in accordance with reason, God willed that external proofs of his Revelation should be joined to the internal helps of the Holy Spirit."[29] Thus the miracles of Christ and the saints, prophecies, the Church's growth and holiness, and her fruitfulness and stability "are the most certain signs of divine Revelation, adapted to the intelligence of all"; they are "motives of credibility" (*motiva credibilitatis*), which show that the assent of faith is "by no means a blind impulse of the mind."[30]    *1063  2465  548  812*

157. Faith is *certain.* It is more certain than all human knowledge because it is founded on the very word of God who cannot lie. To be sure, revealed truths can seem obscure to human reason and experience, but "the certainty that the divine light gives is greater than that which the light of natural reason gives."[31] "Ten thousand difficulties do not make one doubt."[32]    *2088*

Italics highlight key points

158. "Faith *seeks understanding*":[33] it is intrinsic to faith that a believer desires to know better the One in whom he has put his faith and to understand better what He has revealed: a more penetrating knowledge will in turn call forth a greater faith, increasingly set afire by love. The grace of faith opens "the eyes of your hearts"[34] to a lively understanding of the contents of Revelation: that is, of the totality of God's plan and the mysteries of faith, of their connection with each other and with Christ, the centre of the revealed mystery. "The same Holy Spirit constantly perfects faith by his gifts, so that    *2705  1827  90*

The text shows how all the elements of the faith flow from God's plan, with Christ as the centre

---

26 *Dei Filius* 3: DS 3008.
27 St Thomas Aquinas, *STh* II-II, 2, 9; cf. *Dei Filius* 3: DS 3010.
28 *Dei Filius* 3: DS 3008.
29 *Dei Filius* 3: DS 3009.
30 *Dei Filius* 3: DS 3008-10; cf. *Mk* 16:20; *Heb* 2:4.
31 St Thomas Aquinas, *STh* II-II, 171, 5, obj. 3.
32 John Henry Cardinal Newman, *Apologia pro vita sua* (London: Longman, 1878), 239.
33 St Anselm, *Prosl.* prooem.: PL 153, 225A.
34 *Eph* 1:18.

**Christ's true body**

476. Since the Word became flesh in assuming a true humanity, Christ's body was finite.[112] Therefore the human face of Jesus can be portrayed; at the seventh ecumenical council (Nicaea II in 787) the Church recognized its representation in holy images to be legitimate.[113]

477. At the same time the Church has always acknowledged that in the body of Jesus "we recognize in him God made visible, [so that] we may be caught up through him in the love of things invisible."[114] The individual characteristics of Christ's body express the divine person of God's Son. He has made the features of his human body his own, to the point that they can be venerated when portrayed in a holy image, for the believer "who venerates the icon is venerating in it the person of the one depicted."[115]

**The heart of the Incarnate Word**

478. Jesus knew and loved us each and all during his life, his agony and his Passion and gave himself up for each one of us: "The Son of God... loved me and gave himself for me."[116] He has loved us all with a human heart. For this reason, the Sacred Heart of Jesus, pierced by our sins and for our salvation,[117] "is quite rightly considered the chief sign and symbol of that love with which the divine Redeemer continually loves the eternal Father and all human beings" without exception.[118]

## IN BRIEF

479. *At the time appointed by God, the only Son of the Father, the eternal Word, that is, the Word and substantial Image of the Father, became incarnate; without losing his divine nature he has assumed human nature.*

480. *Jesus Christ is true God and true man, in the unity of his divine person; for this reason he is the one and only mediator between God and men.*

481. *Jesus Christ possesses two natures, one divine and the other human, not confused, but united in the one person of God's Son.*

482. *Christ, being true God and true man, has a human intellect and will, perfectly attuned and subject to his divine intellect and divine will, which he has in common with the Father and the Holy Spirit.*

483. *The Incarnation is therefore the mystery of the wonderful union of the divine and human natures in the one person of the Word.*

---

[112] Cf. Council of the Lateran (649): DS 504.
[113] Cf. *Gal* 3:1; cf. Council of Nicaea II (787): DS 600-603.
[114] *Roman Missal*, Preface I of the Nativity of the Lord.
[115] Council of Nicaea II: DS 601.
[116] *Gal* 2:20.
[117] Cf. *Jn* 19:34.
[118] Pius XII, Enc. *Haurietis aquas* (1956): DS 3924; cf. DS 3812.

The whole text is an annunciation of God's love

### Paragraph 2: "Conceived by the Power of the Holy Spirit and Born of the Virgin Mary"

#### I. Conceived by the Power of the Holy Spirit...

The primacy of God's action in our lives is reiterated

484. The Annunciation to Mary inaugurates "the fulness of time",[119] the time of the fulfilment of God's promises and preparations. Mary was invited to conceive him in whom the "whole fulness of deity" would dwell "bodily".[120] The divine response to her question, "How can this be, since I know not man?" was given by the power of the Spirit: "The Holy Spirit will come upon you."[121]

461
721

485. The mission of the Holy Spirit is always conjoined and ordered to that of the Son.[122] The Holy Spirit, "the Lord, the giver of Life", is sent to sanctify the womb of the Virgin Mary and divinely fecundate it, causing her to conceive the eternal Son of the Father in a humanity drawn from her own.

689
723

486. The Father's only Son, conceived as man in the womb of the Virgin Mary, is "Christ", that is to say, anointed by the Holy Spirit, from the beginning of his human existence, though the manifestation of this fact takes place only progressively: to the shepherds, to the magi, to John the Baptist, to the disciples.[123] Thus the whole life of Jesus Christ will make manifest "how God anointed Jesus of Nazareth with the Holy Spirit and with power."[124]

437

#### II...Born of the Virgin Mary

487. What the Catholic faith believes about Mary is based on what it believes about Christ, and what it teaches about Mary illumines in turn its faith in Christ.

96

The *Catechism* emphasises the dignity of the person and our free co-operation with God's plan

#### Mary's predestination

488. "God sent forth his Son,"[125] but to prepare a body for him,[126] he wanted the free co-operation of a creature. For this, from all eternity God chose for the mother of his Son a daughter of Israel, a young Jewish woman of Nazareth in Galilee, "a virgin betrothed to a man whose name was Joseph, of the house of David; and the virgin's name was Mary".[126]

The Father of mercies willed that the Incarnation should be preceded by assent on the part of the predestined mother, so that just as a woman had a share in the coming of death, so also should a woman contribute to the coming of life.[127]

The timeless truths of the faith are presented in the precise and rich language of the Tradition

[119] *Gal* 4:4.
[120] *Col* 2:9.
[121] *Lk* 1:34-35 (Greek).
[122] Cf. *Jn* 16:14-15.
[123] Cf. *Mt* 1:20; 2:1-12; *Lk* 1:35; 2:8-20; *Jn* 1:31-34; 2:11.
[124] *Acts* 10:38.
[125] *Gal* 4:4; *Heb* 10:5.
[126] *Lk* 1:26-27.
[127] *LG* 56; cf. *LG* 61.

# Endnotes

[1] The first edition of the *Catechism of the Catholic Church* (hereafter *CCC*) was published in French on 11th October 1992. It was then translated into various languages and the English edition was published in 1994. The definitive Latin edition, the *editio typica*, of the *Catechismus Catholicae Ecclesiae* was published, after a series of final amendments, on 15th August 1997.

[2] The elements of this craft are explained by Cardinals Schönborn and Ratzinger in their *Introduction to the Catechism of the Catholic Church*, San Francisco, Ignatius Press 1994, and also in the *Prologue* to the *Catechism* itself. The care with which the *Catechism* has been written in order to unlock for us the central truths of the faith and to assist us in communicating these truths to others has also been explained in P. de Cointet, B. Morgan and P. Willey, *The Catechism of the Catholic Church and the Craft of Catechesis*, San Francisco, Ignatius Press 2008.

[3] *Lk* 2:10.

[4] *Lk* 1:38. This response is often abbreviated as Mary's *fiat*, from the Latin "Let it be done". See *CCC* 494, 2617.

[5] *CCC* 722.

[6] *Wis* 18:14-15.

[7] See *CCC* 464.

[8] Pope St John Paul II, Apostolic Exhortation, *Catechesi tradendae* (hereafter *CT*), 20.

[9] As the *Letter to the Ephesians* puts it, so that we attain to "the unity of the faith and of the knowledge of the Son of God, to mature manhood, to the measure of the stature of the fulness of Christ" (4:13).

[10] See *CCC* 429.

[11] The text of the *Catechism*, the result of a collaboration among all of the bishops of the world over a period of seven years, was published as a "sure and authentic reference text" and a "sure norm" for teaching catholic doctrine (see Pope St John Paul II, Apostolic Constitution *Fidei Depositum*).

[12] *CCC* 1694. See *Phil*.2:5.

[13] *CCC* 1694.

[14] *CCC* 2558 (my italics).

[15] *CCC* 1697.

[16] See *CCC* 704; 1104-1107.

[17] *CCC* 1707, citing the Second Vatican Council's *Gaudium et spes* 13.

[18] See *Matt* 28:18-20.

[19] See *CCC* 1717.

[20] See *CCC* 427.

[21] *Summa Theologica* III, 71,4,ad.3, cited in *CCC* 904. See also *CCC* 3.

[22] This is always the pattern, first to receive and then to hand on.

St Paul writes of this in his First Letter to the Corinthians: "For I delivered to you as of first importance what I also received, that Christ..." (*1 Cor* 15:3) We are disciples commissioned by Christ to *learn* and then to *teach*.

[23] Cf. *Eph* 1:17-18.

[24] *CCC* 2677.

[25] Mary is rightly called the "first disciple", wrote St John Paul II, because "no one has been 'taught by God' (*Jn* 6:45) to such depth." (*CT* 73)

[26] Because "Mary is Mother of God and our mother" she "gives us Jesus, her son". This in turn enables us to entrust ourselves to her and to join ourselves to her action and her abandonment to the Father's saving will. See *CCC* 2677.

[27] *CCC* 429.

[28] In the New Testament, Timothy was urged to "guard" this deposit (see *1 Tim* 6:20).

[29] *Lk* 2:19.

[30] See *CCC* 188. For a discussion of how the name *symbolon* came to be attached to the Creed, see J.N.D. Kelly, *Early Christian Creeds*, 3rd edition, London, Longman 1972, pp.52-61.

[31] *Expl. symb.* 8: PL 17, 1196, cited in *CCC* 197. See also *CCC* 94 which, in speaking of the growth in the Church of the understanding of the great heritage of what God has revealed, refers us to Luke 2:19 and 2:51, to Mary's contemplative pondering as she kept and guarded the truth about her Son in her heart.

[32] In fact, Pope St John Paul II described Mary as a "living catechism" for this reason. See *CT* 73. Pope Francis speaks of Mary in a similar fashion: "She appears to us as a vessel filled to the brim with the memory of Jesus, as the Seat of Wisdom to whom we can have recourse to understand his teaching aright." (*Homily for the Feast of the Mother of God*, 1st January 2016)

[33] These principles are explained in the *General Directory for Catechesis*, Vatican City, Libreria Editrice Vaticana, 1997. The *Catechism* is the text *par excellence* that enshrines these principles.

[34] For this metaphor see the description of the *Catechism* on the inside front cover. We shall examine the description of the *Catechism* given here in more detail in the next chapter.

[35] For an extended discussion of this image and why it is important see *http://www.usccb.org/beliefs-and-teachings/how-we-teach/catechesis/catechetical-sunday/year-of-faith/teaching-aid-willey.cfm*.

[36] *Confessions*, Book 10: 20, 29, cited in *CCC* 1718.

[37] It is worth noting that a papal saint has been closely involved in the publication of each: St Pius V for the *Roman Catechism* and St John Paul II for the *Catechism* in our own day. In addition, St Charles

Borromeo was a prominent figure in the work of bringing the *Roman Catechism* to birth.

[38] *Acts* 2:42.

[39] *CCC* 3. My italics.

[40] *CCC* 11,18.

[41] We will examine this point about the major themes in Chapter 4.

[42] *CCC* 13.

[43] See, for example, *1 Cor* 3:9ff; *Matt* 21:42; *Eph* 2:19-22. Cf. *CCC* 756.

[44] *1 Tim* 3:15.

[45] *Ps* 11:3.

[46] C. Schönborn and J. Ratzinger, *Introduction to the Catechism of the Catholic Church*, p.46.

[47] *CCC* 2565.

[48] See C. Schönborn and J. Ratzinger, Ibid, pp.48-49. For a discussion of this point see also P. de Cointet, B. Morgan and P. Willey, *The Catechism of the Catholic Church and the Craft of Catechesis*, pp.19-22.

[49] See *CCC* 830.

[50] For St Thomas see *CCC* 1718, for St Teresa see *CCC* 222.

[51] For the interpretation of this image see the text reproduced on the inside front cover of the *Catechism*.

[52] The *Compendium* was written in order to provide the contents of the *Catechism* in a more abbreviated way and in a question and answer format. It is intended to lead people to the *Catechism* itself and provides constant references to the full *Catechism*. One striking feature of the *Compendium* is that it has increased further the use of images: there are fourteen in total, summing up different parts and sections of the text.

[53] See *Col* 1:15; *Jn* 1:1ff.

[54] *CCC* 2715.

[55] The *Compendium* reinforces this same strong message of Christ-centredness through its use of an icon of *Christ the Pantocrator* at the beginning of the work.

[56] Following Jewish tradition, the Lord's authoritative teaching is given seated (see, for example, *Matt* 5:1; 7:28-29; *Lk* 5:3).

[57] *Num* 24:17.

[58] See *CCC* 1697, 1966, 2074.

[59] *Compendium*, Introduction, 5.

[60] *CCC* 2503.

[61] *1 Jn* 1:1.

[62] See *CCC* 108.

[63] *CCC* 1159.

[64] St John Damascene, *De imag.* 1,16: PG 96:1245A, in *CCC* 1159.

[65] Gerard Manley Hopkins, "As kingfishers catch fire, dragonflies dráw fláme".

[66] *CCC* 2705.

[67] *Tota pulchra* means "total beauty" or "beautiful" and is a phrase used for Jesus and for Mary, the one who received Jesus fully into her life.

[68] *Compendium*, Introduction, 5.

[69] See, for example, *CCC* 1158, 1162, 1181. For the original harmony of the person in all of his dimensions see *CCC* 374-379. "Harmony" is the key concept in this presentation of the state of being of our first parents.

[70] *Compendium*, Introduction, 5.

[71] Pius XII, "The Function of Art", An address to a group of Italian artists received in audience on 8th April 1952.

[72] Cf. *De Musica*, VI, 13, 38: PL 32, 1183-1184; *Confessiones*, IV, 13.20: PL 32, 7.

[73] Pope Francis, *Evangelii Gaudium*, 167.

[74] *Revelations of Divine Love*, trans. James Walsh SJ, London, Burns and Oates, 1961, Ch.5. A quotation from this work is included in the *Catechism*, *CCC* 313.

[75] *Is* 40:15.

[76] *CCC* 52, referring to *1 Tim* 6:16.

[77] For this description see *CCC* 704.

[78] See *CCC* 1691, 1696.

[79] *CCC* 89.

[80] *CCC* 2051.

[81] *CCC* 873.

[82] *Jn* 17:3; *1 Tim* 2:3-4; *Acts* 4:12.

[83] *Jn* 1:18; see *CCC* 151.

[84] This section is *CCC* 199-267.

[85] *CCC* 234.

[86] "Mystery" is a term that refers to God and the things of God. The "mysteries of the faith" are those things we know about because God has chosen to reveal them to us (for example, the sacraments). They are "mysteries" because they concern God whom we can truly know but whose infinite depths we can never plumb.

[87] Following on from the symphonic image that we saw to be so important to the *Catechism*'s structure, it is interesting to note that the centre of the classical symphony, as of all tonal work, lies in a triad (a three-note chord). See C. Rosen, *The Classical Style: Haydn, Mozart, Beethoven*, London, Faber and Faber, 1971, pp.23-25. Similarly, the "harmony" of the faith lies in the unified work of the three Persons: see *CCC* 258-259.

[88] See *CCC* 1693-1695.

[89] *CCC* 2565.

[90] *CCC* 50.

[91] *CCC* 1.
[92] See *CCC* 6.
[93] *CCC* 53-67.
[94] See, for example, among the many references, *CCC* 705, 1040, 1066. The term "economy" was originally related to the notion of the oversight of a household. God's "economy" is his loving plan for the care of the household of creation. Gradually, in secular use, the term has become narrowed to mean the financial aspects of such oversight.
[95] *CCC* 1691.
[96] In addition, some of the treatments of individual doctrines emphasise this point anew. See, for example, the presentations on the angels (*CCC* 332-336), the Holy Spirit (*CCC* 683-747) and the Church (*CCC* 758-769).
[97] The opening paragraph of Part Two is not difficult for an English person to commit to memory: *CCC* 1066!
[98] See *CCC* 2566-2649.
[99] *CCC* 221.
[100] *CCC* 27, citing Vatican Council II, *Gaudium et spes* 19,1. My italics.
[101] Ibid.
[102] *CCC* 2697.
[103] *CCC* 2668.
[104] *CCC* 2565.
[105] *CCC* 1707, citing Vatican Council II, *Gaudium et spes* 13,2.
[106] *CCC* 1769.
[107] *CCC* 1695.
[108] *CCC* 2114.
[109] *CCC* 18.
[110] *CCC* 2575.
[111] Elsewhere St John Paul II emphasised this crucial connection between learning the faith organically and the unity of the person. He wrote, "I wish to reaffirm strongly the conviction that the human being can come to a unified and organic intellectual vision. ...The segmentation of knowledge, with its splintered approach to truth and consequent fragmentation, keeps people today from coming to an interior unity." (*Fides et ratio*, 85)
[112] *CCC* 795.
[113] *CCC* 845.
[114] See *CCC* 1702, 1878-1880.
[115] The sources are of two kinds: direct quotations, provided in the main text, and then further references for additional enrichment, the latter indicated by the 'cf.' in the source reference. These latter sources have been usefully gathered in a single volume, the *Companion to the Catechism of the Catholic Church*, San Francisco,

Ignatius Press 1993. An abbreviations key to the sources is found at the beginning of the *Catechism*.

[116] In the New Testament index you will see that only seven chapters are not explicitly included there. In other words, almost every chapter from every book of the New Testament has informed the text of the *Catechism*.

[117] This image is used by Frank Sheed, the English apologist and publisher, in his work, *Are We Really Teaching Religion?* (London, Sheed and Ward, 1953, p.9) to describe the familiarity he hoped every teacher of the Catholic faith would have with the Scriptures and their contents.

[118] J.Ratzinger, *Gospel, Catechesis, Catechism*, San Francisco, Ignatius Press, 1977, p.61.

[119] See *CCC* 101-141.

[120] *CCC* 122.

[121] See *CCC* 128-130.

[122] *CCC* 124, citing Vatican Council II, *Dei Verbum*, 18.

[123] *CCC* 126, citing *Dei Verbum* 19.

[124] See, for example, *CCC* 498, 639, 646.

[125] See *CCC* 115-119. For a discussion of the spiritual sense of the Scriptures see Joseph Ratzinger, 'Sources and transmission of the faith', *Communio* 10(1), Spring 1983, pp.17-34.

[126] *Eph* 1:3.

[127] See *Rom* 1:5; 16:26.

[128] *CCC* 143.

[129] *CCC* 144-149.

[130] *CCC* 146.

[131] *CCC* 148.

[132] *CCC* 65, quoting from St John of the Cross, *The Ascent of Mount Carmel* 2, 22, 3f.

[133] *CCC* 1085.

[134] *CCC* 1099; cf. *Jn* 14:26.

[135] *Rom* 12:2.

[136] *CCC* 171.

[137] *CCC* 106, citing *Dei Verbum* 11.

[138] *CCC* 1071.

[139] *CCC* 2564. My italics.

[140] See *CCC* 306-307.

[141] *CCC* 969.

[142] *CCC* 967.

[143] *CCC* 956, citing Vatican Council II, *Lumen Gentium*, 49.

[144] *CCC* 25.

[145] See *CCC* 1402, citing Eucharistic Prayer I (the Roman Canon).

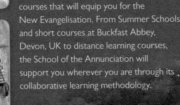